Hurt To Healing
Transformation Center

Study Guide And Workbook

Hurt To Healing
Transformation Center

Study Guide And Workbook

GAIL HURT

Copyright 2024 by PIAOTT Publishing & Graphic Design LLC.

All rights reserved. This book or any portion thereof may not be reproduced or used in any manner whatsoever without the express written permission of the publisher except for the use of brief quotations in a book review.

PIAOTT Publishing & Graphic Design LLC.

Chicago, Illinois

Print ISBN: 979-8-9892562-4-2

DEDICATION

*To all the brave women on the path from hurt to healing,
this workbook is dedicated to you. Each story, each struggle, and
each triumph matters. May these pages be a safe space for
reflection, growth, and transformation.*

*As we support one another through the healing process,
may we find strength in our shared experiences and the courage
to embrace the journey ahead.*

Together, we will rise, heal, and reclaim our power.

Table of Contents

Introduction: 1

Session 1: Understanding the Hurt 3

Session 2: The Impact of Hurt 15

Session 3: The Healing Journey 25

Session 4: Emotional Expression 35

Session 5: Self-Compassion and Forgiveness 49

Session 6: Recognize Healing From Past Hurts and Trauma 59

Session 7: Avoid Being A Dumping Ground During
          Your Healing Process 67

Session 8: Support Systems 75

Biography & Testimonials: 79

She is like a tree planted by streams of water that yields its fruit in its season, and its leaf does not wither. In all that She does, She prospers.

An adaptation of Psalm 1:3 NIV

Hurt to Healing
Transformation Center
Study Guide & Workbook

Introduction

In today's fast-paced world, the importance of fostering supportive environments for women to express themselves cannot be understated. Hurt to Healing Transformation Center is all about initiating and creating a safe space for women to come together in a small group setting, where they can share their experiences, challenges, and triumphs without fear and judgment or backlash. This initiative recognizes that open dialogue and peer support can significantly enhance mental well-being, empower individual voices, and build a sense of community among participants.

This group will provide structured sessions that promote trust and confidentiality, ensuring that every woman feels valued and heard. We will implement guidelines that encourage respect and active listening, creating a nurturing atmosphere where everyone can engage meaningfully.

By participating in this program, women will not only have the opportunity to articulate their thoughts and feelings but also to learn from one another, fostering personal growth and collective strength. Ultimately, our goal is to cultivate a vibrant network of support that enhances resilience and empowers women to thrive both personally and professionally.

The Journey from Hurt to Healing

The journey from hurt to healing is a profound and transformative experience, one that often begins in a place of deep personal turmoil. It is in the shadows of pain that we frequently find ourselves grappling with our worth and seeking solace in a world that feels overwhelming. This initial phase can be marked by feelings of isolation and despair, as we confront the wounds that have shaped our lives. Acknowledging this hurt is crucial; it serves as the catalyst for change, reminding us that healing requires not only time but also willingness to confront the past.

As we embark on the path toward healing, we gradually learn to navigate our emotions with greater resilience. This phase is characterized by self-discovery and the pursuit of inner strength. We begin to develop coping strategies and seek support from others, whether through therapy, community, or self-reflection. With each step taken, we transform our pain into a source of empowerment, ultimately embracing a new narrative of hope and renewal. Healing is not a linear journey; rather, it is a complex evolution that teaches us the value of compassion for ourselves and others, paving the way for a future filled with possibility and growth.

Session

1

Understanding the Hurt

Session 1

Identifying Sources of Pain

Identifying the sources of pain from trauma and past hurts requires a nuanced understanding of both the physical and emotional dimensions of injury. Physical trauma, whether due to accidents, falls, or other direct impacts, can result in immediate, acute pain or lead to long-term chronic discomfort. When examining pain from physical trauma, it's important to first consider the nature of the injury. Bruises, fractures, sprains and strains all produce distinct patterns of pain, often characterized by swelling, tenderness, or limited range of motion in the affected area. Sometimes trauma can cause deeper injuries like nerve damage or soft tissue injuries, which might not be immediately apparent but can lead to lasting pain, numbness, or a tingling sensation. Imaging tools like X-rays, MRIs, and CT scans can help reveal the underlying physical damage and assist in diagnosing the source of pain.

In contrast, emotional and psychological trauma often presents a more complex challenge when identifying pain. Past hurts, such as childhood abuse, the loss of a loved one, or unresolved grief, can leave deep emotional scars that manifest physically over time. The body often stores emotional pain, and many people experience what's known as somatic symptoms-physical manifestations of emotional distress, such as chronic headaches, backs pain, or gastrointestinal issues. This mind-body connection can make it difficult to differentiate between pain originating from physical injury and pain tied to emotional wounds. In some cases, a person who has experienced trauma may report pain in areas that don't show physical injury but where they feel a sense of emotional tension or distress. For example, someone who has experienced emotional abuse may experience tightness in their chest or shoulders, even if no apparent physical injury exists.

Unresolved emotional pain can also create a cycle where past traumas cause ongoing physical pain. Psychological conditions like post-traumatic stress disorder (PTSD), anxiety, and depression are often linked to chronic physical symptoms, making it essential for healthcare providers to take a holistic approach when assessing pain. Techniques such as trauma-informed care, which considers emotional and psychological history, are crucial in identifying and addressing these kinds of pain. The effects of past trauma can linger in the body and the mind, influencing how one experiences pain and how it is processed.

Ultimately, recognizing the sources of pain from past trauma requires an integrated approach that accounts for both the physical and emotional components. This can involve detailed questioning about past experiences, including any history of abuse, injury, or loss, alongside a thorough physical examination.

Addressing the roots of pain, whether they lie in the body or the psyche, is often the first step toward effective treatment, which may include a combination of physical therapy, psychotherapy, or a combination of both.

Discussion on Different Types of Hurt

EMOTIONAL HURT – This can stem from experiences such as loss, rejection, betrayal, or trauma. Some root causes can be hereditary, problems caused by schoolmates, being adopted or factors in the family home. Emotional hurt can lead to various feelings, including sadness, anger, confusion, depression, disappointment, low self esteem and anxiety.

Suggestions for coping

- **Acknowledge your Feelings** – Recognize and accept your emotions as a valid response to your experiences.
- **Talk About It** – Expressing your feelings to a trusted friend, family member, or therapist can provide relief and perspective.
- **Journaling** – Writing down your thoughts and feelings can help you process your emotions and gain clarity.
- **Self-Care** – Engage in activities that promote your well-being, such as exercise, meditation, or hobbies that you enjoy.
- **Seek Professional Help** – If emotional hurt is overwhelming or persistent, consider talking to a mental health professional for support.

RELATIONSHIP HURT – Refers to the emotional pain and distress that arises from interactions and relationships with others. This can occur in various contexts, including romantic relationships, friendships, family dynamics, or professional settings. Common causes of relational hurt include misunderstandings, betrayal, lack of communication, rejection, or unresolved conflicts.

Suggestions for coping

- **Identify the Source** – Reflect on what specifically caused the hurt. Understanding the root of your feelings can help in addressing it.

- *Communicate Openly* – If possible, talk to the person involved about your feelings. Honest communication can help clear misunderstandings and promote healing.
- *Establish Boundaries* – Set personal boundaries to protect yourself from further hurt. This might involve limiting contact with certain individuals or redefining the nature of the relationship.

Practice Forgiveness – While it may be difficult, forgiving the person who has hurt you can lead to emotional healing. This doesn't mean excusing their behavior, but rather letting go of the hold it has on you.

Reflect on the Relationship – Sometimes evaluating whether a relationship is healthy or beneficial for you is necessary. It may be time to move on if it consistently causes pain.

PHYSICAL HURT OR ABUSE – Refers to the intentional infliction of bodily harm to another person. This can include acts such as hitting, kicking, slapping, burning, or any other form of physical violence. Physical abuse can occur in various contexts, including intimate relationships, family settings, or even in institutional environments.

Suggestions for coping

- *Reach out for help* – If you are in an abusive situation, it's important to seek help. This could be from friends, family, or support hotlines.
- *Create a Safety Plan* – Plan for a safe place to go if you need to leave an abusive situation quickly.
- *Document Evidence* – Keep records of incidents, including dates,

descriptions of abuse and photographs of injuries, which can be important for legal action or support services.
- **Seek Medical Attention** – If you have been physically harmed, seek medical help for your injuries. This is important for both your health and documentation of abuse.
- **Find Support Services** – Look for local organizations that specialize in helping victims of domestic violence or abuse. They provide resources, shelter, counseling, and legal assistance.
- **Consider Therapy** – Engaging with a mental health professional can help process the trauma associated with being physically abused and promote healing.
- **Know your Rights** – Familiarize yourself with local laws about domestic violence and individuals' rights. Legal aid organizations can help navigate this process.
- *Journaling Exercise*:

Write about personal experiences of hurt:

_____
_____
_____
_____
_____
_____
_____
_____
_____
_____
_____

Session 1 Questions

Please use extra paper if needed.

Personal Reflections:
1. Can you share an experience where you felt hurt in a relationship?
2. What were the circumstances?
3. How did you initially react to this hurt?
4. Did you communicate with the person involved?

Understanding Emotions:
5. What emotions surfaced for you during or after the hurtful experience?
6. How do you cope with feelings of hurt or betrayal in your relationships?

Patterns and Triggers:
7. Have you noticed any patterns in the types of relationships where you feel more hurt?
8. What might these patterns reveal?
9. What triggers feelings of hurt for you in a relationship?

Impact on Relationships:
10. How has relational hurt affected your trust in others moving forward?
11. In what ways has your experience with hurt influenced how you interact with new people?

Healing and Growth:
12. What steps have you taken toward healing from relational hurt in the past?

13. How can we support each other in the healing process from relational pain?

Boundary Setting:

14. How do you establish boundaries in relationships to prevent future hurt?
15. What boundaries have you found to be most helpful in your relationships?

Communication Strategies:

16. What is a healthy way to communicate feelings of hurt to someone without escalating conflict?
17. How do you decide when to confront someone about a hurtful situation?

Lessons Learned:

18. What have you learned about yourself through your experiences of relational hurt?
19. How can past hurt inform how you build healthier relationships in the future?

Support Systems:

20. Who do you turn to for support when dealing with relationship hurt?
21. How can we create a safe space for sharing and healing within our group?

Vision for the Future:

22. What does a healthy relationship look like to you after experiencing hurt?
23. How can we cultivate resilience and foster stronger connections moving forward?

Use the following pages for your answers:

Session

2

The Impact of Hurt

Session 2

Exploring How Hurt Affects Mental and Physical Health

Hurt, whether emotional or physical, can profoundly impact both mental and physical health. Below are some insights into how hurt affect various aspects of well-being.

Emotional Impact

Mood Swings – Individuals may experience heightened emotions, including anger, sadness, or frustration, which can affect daily functioning and relationships.

Isolation – Hurt can lead to social withdrawal as individuals may feel misunderstood or unable to share their experiences, increasing feelings of loneliness.

Mental Health Disorders – Experiencing hurt, especially from trauma or prolonged distress, can lead to anxiety, depression, or post-traumatic stress disorder (PTSD).

Physical Impact:

Stress Response – Hurt triggers the body's stress response, releasing hormones like cortisol. Chronic stress can lead to various physical issues, including headaches, fatigue, and muscle tension.

Immune System – Prolonged emotional pain can weaken the immune system, making a person more susceptible to illnesses.

Chronic Conditions – Emotional distress has been linked to chronic health conditions such as heart disease, diabetes, and gastrointestinal disorders.

Behavioral Changes:

Coping Mechanisms – Individuals may engage in unhealthy coping strategies, such as substance abuse, overeating, or self-harm, leading to further health issues.

Sleep Disturbances- Hurt can disrupt sleep patterns, resulting in insomnia or hypersomnia, which in turn can affect your overall health and well-being.

Social and Cognitive Effects:

Cognitive Functioning- Emotional pain can affect concentration, decision making, and memory, impacting daily activities and productivity.

Strained Relationships – Hurt can create barriers in relationships, leading to misunderstandings, conflicts, or distancing ones from loved ones.

The interplay between emotional and physical health is complex, and addressing both aspects is essential for healing. If you're navigating through hurt, consider reaching out for support or professional help to foster recovery and resilience.

Steps for Healing

- *Therapy and Counseling* – Professional help can provide coping strategies and emotional support,
- *Mindfulness and Meditation* – Practices that promote awareness and relaxation can help manage stress and emotional pain.
- *Support Networks* – Engaging with friends, family, or support

groups can reduce feelings of isolation and provide validation.

▸ *Journaling Exercise*:

Write about the impact of hurt on your daily life:

Session 2 Questions

Please use extra paper if needed.

Physical Impact

Body Awareness:

1. How have experiences of emotional hurt manifested physically in your body (e.g., tension, fatigue, illness)?
2. Have you noticed any changes in your health when you are emotionally hurt, such as changes in appetite or sleep patterns?

Stress and Health:

3. How do you think chronic stress from emotional hurt affects your physical health over time?
4. What physical symptoms do you experience when you're dealing with mental or emotional pain?

Coping Through Activity:

5. In what ways do you use physical activities (like exercise, yoga, or outdoor activities) to cope with emotional hurt?
6. Have you found any physical practices that help alleviate stress resulting from emotional pain?

Seeking Help:

7. Have you ever sought physical treatment (like therapy, massage, or alternative therapies) for symptoms stemming from emotional hurt?
8. What role do you think medical professionals should play in addressing the physical aspects of emotional hurt?

Mental Impact

Emotional Processing:

9. How do you process emotional hurt mentally?
10. Do you have any specific strategies you find helpful?
11. Have you experienced any mental health challenges (like anxiety or depression) due to significant hurt in your life?

Self-Perception:

12. How has emotional hurt influenced your self-esteem and how you talk to yourself?
13. In what ways have you learned to redefine your identity after experiencing pain?

Coping Mechanisms:

14. What mental coping strategies have you found effective when dealing with emotional hurt?
15. How do you deal with negative thoughts that can come from feeling hurt?

Support and Healing:

16. How important is it to you to have a support system when dealing with both physical and mental pain from hurt?
17. What role does sharing your experiences within a group like this play in your healing process?

Holistic Approach

Integrative Healing:

18. How do you view the connection between mental health and physical health when addressing hurt?

19. What holistic practices (like mindfulness, meditation, or therapy) have you found helpful in promoting healing for your mind, body and soul?

Preventative Measures:

20. What steps can be taken to minimize the mental and physical impacts of hurt in our lives?
21. How do you envision building resilience against future hurts that could affect your mental and physical health?
22. These questions encourage a comprehensive exploration of the effects of hurt and may faster deeper connections and understanding among the group members.

Use the following pages for your answers:

Session

3

The Healing Journey

Session 3

Acknowledgment and Acceptance

Acknowledgment and acceptance of feelings are important aspects of emotional intelligence and effective communication. Here are some key points to consider.

- **Acknowledgment** – This involves recognizing and validating both your own feelings as well as those of others. It means saying to yourself or someone else, I see how you feel, or your feelings are valid. This can be crucial in building trust and understanding.

- **Acceptance** – Accepting feelings means allowing those feelings to exist without judgment. Instead of denying or suppressing emotions, you recognize that they are a natural part of being human, and it's okay to feel what you are feeling. This often requires self-compassion and patience.

- **Expressing Feelings** – It helps to articulate feelings openly. Using I statement (like I feel) can create a safe space for communication and reduce defensiveness.

- **Active Listening** – When someone shares their feelings, practice active listening. Give them your full attention, refrain from interrupting, and reflect on what you hear to show understanding.

- **Encouraging Emotional Expression** – Encourage a culture where feelings can be expressed freely without fear of stigma or retribution. It enhances relationships and promote mental well-being.

The Importance of Recognizing Feelings

Recognizing feelings is crucial for several reasons.

- **Emotional Awareness** – Acknowledging your feelings helps develop emotional awareness, allowing you to understand your emotional triggers and responses better. This self-awareness is vital for personal growth and self-regulation.

- **Mental Health** – Recognizing feelings can prevent emotional buildup, leading to anxiety, or depression. By acknowledging emotions, you can process them more effectively and seek appropriate support when needed.

- **Improved Relationships** – Understanding and acknowledging your own feelings can help you to better empathize with others. This fosters healthier communication and strengthens relationships, as people feel heard and valued.

- **Conflict Resolution** – When feelings are recognized, it promotes open dialogue instead of defensiveness, leading to better conflict resolution. People are more likely to work through disagreements when they feel understood.

- **Enhanced Resilience** – Equips you with the tools to cope with challenges more effectively. It encourages adaptive coping strategies and resilience in the face of adversity.

- **Promoting Authenticity** – Expressing your feelings authentically allows you to live more genuinely, aligning your actions with your emotions and values.

Guided Meditation

Guided Meditation for acceptance can help cultivate a mindset of openness and peace, allowing you to embrace your experiences and feelings without judgment. Here's a simple guide to meditation you can follow. Preferably I use Christian Meditation- which involves reflecting on spiritual themes and scriptures to deepen one's relationship With God. It can include various methods such as:

- *Scriptural Meditation:* Focusing on a specific Bible verse or passage, contemplating its meaning and how it applies to one's life.
- *Contemplative Prayer:* Sitting in silence, consciously and inviting God's presence and allowing thoughts and feelings to surface, often using a repeated prayer or phrase.
- *Guided Meditation:* Using resources like books, apps, or recordings that lead you through a meditation focused on Christian themes.
- *Prayerful Silence:* Spending time in quietness, listening for God's voice, rather than speaking to him.
- *Breath Prayer:* Pairing a short prayer or scripture with breathing to help center your thoughts and facilitate a deeper prayer experience.

Benefits of Christian meditation include enhanced spiritual awareness, increased peace, and a greater sense of connection to God. If you're interested in starting to consider allocating a consistent time each day for meditation, creating a conducive environment, and perhaps keeping a journal to reflect on your experiences.

Setting the Scene

- *Find a Comfortable Position* – Sit or lie down in a quiet place where you won't be disturbed. Close your eyes if you feel comfortable doing so.

- *Take a Deep Breath* – Inhale deeply through your nose, filling your lungs. Hold for a moment, then exhale slowly through your mouth. Repeat this a few times to ground yourself.

How To Meditate

Focus on the Present – Bring awareness to your breath. Notice the natural rhythm of your breathing. The rise and fall of your chest or belly. Allow your breath to become your anchor.

- *Acknowledge your Feelings* – As you breathe, invite any feelings or thoughts that arise to come into your awareness. There's no need to change them; simply acknowledge their presence. You might say to yourself, I see you, and I know you are there.
- *Visualize Acceptance* – Imagine a warm, golden light surrounding you. With each inhale, visualize this light filling you with warmth and comfort. With each exhale, imagine letting go of any resistance or judgment about your feelings.
- *Repeat Affirmations* – Silently or aloud, repeat affirmations of acceptance: I accept myself just as I am. I embrace my feelings without judgment. I release the need to control my experiences.
- *Stay in the Moment* – Continue to breathe deeply and focus on the sensations in your body. Accept whatever arises in this moment, whether it's discomfort, peace, or even uncertainty.
- *Transition to Gratitude* – Shift your focus to gratitude. Think of something in your life that you appreciate. It could be a person, an experience, or even something simple. Allow this feeling of gratitude to fill your heart.

Closing the Meditation

- *Gradually Return* – Bring awareness back to your breath. Notice how your body feels. Wiggle your fingers and toes, and when you're ready, gently open your eyes.

- **Reflect** – Take a moment to reflect on your experience. How do you feel now compared to when started? Remember acceptance is a practice, and it's okay to revisit these feelings whenever you need to.

You can practice this meditation regularly to deepen your sense of acceptance and foster a more compassionate relationship with yourself and your experiences. Feel free to adapt the meditation to your preferences and needs.

Write your favorite scripture, prayer or quote:

Session 3 Questions

Please use extra paper if needed.

Acknowledgment

Personal Reflection:

1. What does acknowledgment mean to you in your personal journey?
2. Can you identify a moment when acknowledging your feelings or experiences was particularly important for you?

Understanding Emotions:

3. How do you differentiate between acknowledging emotions and allowing them to control you?
4. Have you experienced resistance to acknowledging certain feelings or events?
5. What has that been like?

Sharing Stories:

6. How does sharing your story with others help you in acknowledging your experiences?
7. Can you recall a time when you felt truly heard and validated?
8. What impact did it have on you?

Cultural Influences:

9. How do cultural or societal expectations influence your ability to acknowledge your feelings?
10. In what ways can we challenge societal norms that discourage emotional acknowledgment?

Acceptance

The Process of Acceptance:

11. What does acceptance look like for you, and how has it evolved over time?

12. Can you share an experience where acceptance led to personal growth or healing?

Self-Compassion:

13. How does practicing selfcompassion tie into your journey of acceptance?

14. What strategies do you use to cultivate self-acceptance in challenging situations?

Overcoming Barriers:

15. What barriers have you faced in accepting certain aspects of yourself or your experiences?

16. How can we support one another in breaking down these barriers within the group?

17. Living Authentically:

18. How does acceptance of your emotions and experiences empower you to live more authentically?

19. In what ways have you noticed that acceptance alters your relationships with others?

Growth and Empowerment

Facilitating Change:

20. How can acknowledgment and acceptance act as catalysts for change in your life?

21. What role do you believe forgiveness (of yourself or others) plays in the acceptance process?

Encouraging Others:

22. How can we encourage each other to embrace acknowledgment and acceptance in our daily lives?
23. What resources (books, workshops, etc.) have you found helpful in your journey toward acceptance?

Use the following pages for your answers:

Session

4

Emotional Expression

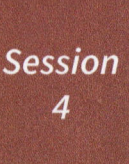

Session 4

Emotional expression refers to the ways we communicate and convey our feelings and emotions, both verbally and non- verbally. It's a vital aspect of human interaction and can take many forms. Here are some key points about emotional expression.

Forms of Emotional Expression

- Verbal Expression – This includes spoken or written words where individuals articulate their feelings (saying I feel sad or writing in a journal).

- Non-Verbal Expression – Body language, facial expressions, gestures, and tone of voice convey emotions. For example, a smile can show happiness, while crossed arms may indicate defensiveness.

- Artistic Expression – Many people express emotions through art, music, dance, or other creative outlets. These forms can help explore and communicate complex feelings.

- Physical Expression – Engaging in physical activities, like sports or exercise, can also be a way of expressing feelings, especially anger and excitement.

Barriers to Emotional Expression

- Social Norms – In some cultures, expressing certain emotions may be frowned upon, leading individuals to suppress feelings.

- Fear of Judgement – People may hesitate to express emotions due to fear of being misunderstood or judged by others
- Lack of Skills – Some may not have learned effective ways to articulate their emotions or may struggle to identify what they are feeling.

Encouraging Healthy Emotional Expression

- Practice Mindfulness – This helps in becoming more aware of your feelings, making it easier to express them.
- Develop Communication Skills – Learning to articulate feelings clearly can enhance emotional expression. Using "I" statements (I feel rather than "You make me feel") can decrease defensiveness.
- Create a Safe Environment – Surround yourself with people who encourage openness and validate your emotions.
- Engage in Creative Outlets – Explore art, music, or writing as ways to express what you might find difficult to say outright.

Emotional expression is essential for personal well-being and healthy relationships. By understanding its forms and overcoming barriers, individuals can improve their emotional intelligence and foster deeper connections with others.

How do you express yourself?

Session 4 Questions - A

Please use extra paper if needed.

Understanding Emotional Expressions

Personal Experience:

1. How do you typically express your emotions? Are there certain emotions you find easier or more difficult to express?
2. Can you share a specific moment when you felt your emotional expression was notably impactful (positively or negatively)?

Cultural Influences:

3. How has your upbringing or cultural background influenced the way you?
4. express (or suppress) your emotions?
5. In what ways do societal norms affect how women are expected to express their emotions?

Communication Styles:

6. Do you feel you communicate your emotions verbally or non-verbally?
7. Which do you find more effective or natural?
8. How do you adapt your emotional expressions in different settings (e.g., at work, with friends, or family)?

Emotional Awareness and Regulation

Identifying Emotions:

9. How do you recognize and label your emotions when they arise? Do you have specific techniques for this?

10. Are there particular triggers that lead you to express emotions more intensely?

Managing Emotions:

11. What strategies do you use to manage overwhelming emotions? How do you ensure you express them healthily?

12. Have you found practices, like mindfulness or journaling, beneficial in understanding your emotional expressions?

Impact on Relationships

Expressing Vulnerability:

13. How comfortable are you with showing vulnerability in your emotional expressions?

14. What fears might you have about being vulnerable?

15. Can you discuss how emotional expressions affect your relationships with friends, family, and partners?

Navigating Conflict:

16. How do you handle conflict when emotions are high?

17. What has worked for you in resolving misunderstandings?

18. Have you ever felt that expressing a particular emotion led to a significant change in a relationship? How so?

Growth and Support

Encouraging Expression:

19. What are some ways we can create a supportive environment for ourselves and each other to express our emotions freely?

20. How can we encourage younger generations of women to express their emotions openly and healthily?

Resource Sharing:

21. Are there books, workshops, or resources you have found helpful in exploring emotional expression?
22. How can we incorporate creative outlets (art, writing, etc.) into our emotional expression practices?

Reflection and Future Goals

Setting Intentions:

23. What intention would you like to set for your emotional expression moving forward?
24. How can this group support you in achieving your goals around emotional expression?

Use the following pages for your answers:

Creative Expression Exercise

Building Resilience

Building resilience is the process of developing the ability to adapt well in the face of adversity, trauma, tragedy, threats, or significant sources of stress. Here are some key strategies to help build resilience.

- Develop a Strong Support Network – Cultivate relationships with family, friends, and colleagues. Support from others can provide comfort and assistance during tough times.
- Practice Self-Care – Prioritize your physical and mental health. Engage in regular exercise, maintain a balanced diet, get enough sleep, and practice mindfulness or meditation.
- Set Realistic Goals – Break your goals into smaller, manageable steps. Celebrate achievements along the way, no matter how small.
- Stay Flexible – Be open to change and willing to adjust your plans. Resilience involves being able to adapt to changing circumstances.
- Learn Problem Solving Skills – Develop critical thinking and problem-solving abilities to handle challenges as they arise effectively.
- Maintain a Positive Outlook – Focus on positive thinking and keep a hopeful attitude. Practice gratitude to help shift your perspective.
- Embrace Learning from Experiences – View setbacks as opportunities to learn and grow. Reflect on past experiences for insights that can aid in future challenges.

- Again, Seek Help When Needed – Don't hesitate to reach out for professional help if you're struggling. Therapy and counseling can be valuable resources.

Building resilience is an ongoing process that takes time and effort. By implementing these strategies, you can enhance your ability to cope with life's challenges.

Session 4 Questions - B

Please use extra paper if needed.

Understanding Resilience

Personal Definition:

1. What does resilience mean to you? How do you define it in your own life?
2. Can you share a time in your life when you felt particularly resilient?
3. What helped you navigate that experience?

Resilience Factors:

4. What personal qualities or strengths do you believe contribute to your resilience?
5. How have your life experiences shaped your ability to cope with adversity?

Coping Strategies

Building Coping Mechanisms:

6. What strategies do you use to cope with stress or difficult situations?

7. Are there particular routines or practices (e.g., mindfulness, exercise, journaling) that help you build resilience?

Seeking Support:

8. How do you reach out for support during challenging times?
9. Who do you rely on for encouragement and guidance?
10. Have you found any mentors or role models who inspire you in terms of resilience?
11. What have you learned from them?

Overcoming Challenges

Facing Adversity:

12. What challenges have you faced that tested your resilience?
13. How did you respond to those challenges?
14. Can you share a lesson learned fram a setback that ultimately strengthened your resilience?

Mindset Shifts:

15. How do you practice shifting your mindset during tough times?
16. Are there affirmations or thought patterns that help you?
17. What role does selfcompassion play in your ability to bounce back from adversity?

Community and Connection

Creating a Resilient Community:

18. In what ways can we create a supportive community that fosters resilience among women?
19. How does sharing experiences with other women contribute

to your own resilience?

Celebrating Strengths:

20. How can we celebrate each other's strengths and resilience within this group?

21. What are some small victories or milestones that you would like to share and celebrate with the group?

Growth and Development

Setting Resilience Goals:

22. What specific goals related to resilience would you like to work on?

23. How can this group help you achieve them?

24. Are there skills or areas of growth you would like to develop that would enhance your resilience?

Reflection and Future Planning:

25. Looking back at your experiences, how do you think you have grown in your resilience?

26. What are some key takeaways?

27. How do you envision using your resilience in future challenges?

28. What future challenges do you foresee, and how can you prepare for them?

Use the following pages for your answers:

Session

5

Self-Compassion And Forgiveness

Session 5

Self-Compassion and Forgiveness are important aspects of emotional well- being that can positively impact mental health and personal growth. Here's a closer look at both concepts.

Self-Compassion

Is defined as treating yourself with kindness, understanding, and support during difficult times such as moments of failure, distress, or suffering. It consists of three main components.

- *Self-Kindness* – Being gentle and understanding toward yourself rather than harshly critical. This means speaking to yourself in the same way you would to a good friend.
- *Common Humanity* – Acknowledging that everyone experiences difficulties and failures. Realizing that you're not alone in your struggles can help reduce feelings of isolation.
- *Mindfulness* – Maintaining a balanced awareness of your emotions. Mindfulness encourages you to observe your feelings without over identifying with them or suppressing them.

Forgiveness

Forgiveness is the process of letting go of anger, resentment, or desire for revenge toward someone who has hurt you, including yourself. Key aspects of forgiveness include.

- *Recognition of Feelings* – Acknowledge and accept your feelings of hurt or anger without judgement. This is an important step to your healing.

Understanding the Impact – Reflect on how holding onto resentment affects your well-being and relationships. Recognizing this may motivate you to forgive.

Choosing to Forgive – This is an active decision, not just a passive feeling. It's about letting go of negative emotions tied to the person or situation.

Self-Forgiveness – Just as you might forgive others, it's crucial to forgive yourself for past mistakes. This allows you to move forward.

Cultivate Compassion for Yourself

When feeling guilty or ashamed, practice self-compassion by acknowledging your feelings and reminding yourself that everyone makes mistakes.

Forgive Yourself

When you forgive yourself, you create space for growth and allow yourself to learn from past experiences rather than being defined by them. Again, incorporating self-compassion and forgiveness into your life can lead to improved emotional health, stronger relationships, and greater resilience.

Forgive yourself for:

_____
_____
_____
_____
_____
_____
_____

Session 5 Questions

Please use extra paper if needed.

Understanding Self-Compassion and Forgiveness

Personal Interpretation:

1. How do you define self-compassion?
2. What does it look like in practice for you?
3. What does forgiveness mean to you, both in terms of forgiving others and yourself?

Importance of Self-Compassion:

4. Why do you believe self-compassion is important for your well-being?
5. Can you share an experience where selfcompassion helped you navigate a difficult situation?

Practicing Self-Compassion

Self-Compassion Techniques:

6. What practices or techniques do you use to cultivate self-compassion in your life?
7. How do you remind yourself to be kind and gentle during challenging times?

Overcoming Self-Judgment:

8. What inner dialogues or self-criticisms do you struggle with?
9. How do you counteract them?
10. Can you share examples of how you have turned negative self-talk into a more compassionate narrative?

Exploring Forgiveness

Forgiveness Journeys:

11. Can you share a situation in which you found it difficult to forgive someone?
12. What made it challenging?
13. How has forgiving someone in your life transformed your perspective or emotional state?

Forgiving Yourself:

14. What are some things you've struggled to forgive yourself for?
15. How have those feelings impacted you?
16. Can you describe a moment when you finally offered yourself forgiveness?
17. What led to that breakthrough?

Linking Self-Compassion and Forgiveness

Connection Between Concepts:

18. How do you think selfcompassion and forgiveness are interconnected?
19. How can one enhance the other?
20. In your experience, how can being self-compassionate help you be more forgiving towards others?

Barriers to Forgiveness:

21. What barriers do you feel are preventing you from forgiving yourself or others?
22. How might self-compassion help you overcome these barriers?

Community and Support

Creating a Supportive Environment:

23. How can this group support each other in practicing self-compassion and forgiveness?

24. In what ways can sharing our experiences of selfcompassion and forgiveness foster a sense of community among us?

Moving Forward:

25. What commitments can we make to ourselves to nurture self-compassion and the practice of forgiveness in our daily lives?

26. What are some goals you would like to set regarding your self-compassion or forgiveness journey?

27. How can this group help you achieve them?

Use the following pages for your answers:

Affirmation Exercises

Create Affirmations - Write down positive statements that resonate with you, such as "I am capable of achieving my goals" or "I deserve love and happiness".

Morning Affirmation Ritual – Start your day by reading your affirmations aloud in front of a mirror. This reinforces positive beliefs about yourself. Try some of these:

- I am strong, capable, and resilient
- I embrace my uniqueness
- I am worthy of love and respect from myself and others
- I have the power to create the life I desire
- I am confident in my abilities and trust my instincts
- I attract positivity and abundance into my life
- I choose to let go of negativity and embrace joy
- I am constantly growing and evolving into my best self

Visualization – While repeating your affirmations, visualize yourself embracing the qualities or outcomes you desire. Picture yourself succeeding in your goals.

Gratitude Affirmations – Combine affirmations with gratitude by expressing what you are thankful for. For example, "I am grateful for my health and ability to pursue my passions.

Weekly Affirmations Review – Review and update your affirmations regularly. Reflect on which ones resonate with you and let go of those that no longer serve you.

Combine Both

Try writing a reflective piece on how your affirmations influence your thoughts and actions. This can help solidify the connection between your self-reflection and the positive changes you wish to foster in your life.

Session

6

Recognizing Healing From Past Hurts And Trauma

Session 6

Healing from past hurts and trauma is a deeply personal journey, and recognizing the signs of healing can vary from person to person. While the process is often nonlinear and comes with its own set of challenges, there are several indicators that can help individuals understand their progress in healing.

Emotional Stability – One of the most significant signs of healing is emotional stability. Individuals who have begun to heal often find that their moods are less volatile. They may experience emotions related to their past traumas, but these feelings are generally less intense or debilitating. For instance, when reminded of the trauma, a healed person might feel sadness or anger but can manage these emotions without being overwhelmed.

Improved Relationships – Healing often leads to healthier relationships. Those who have addressed their past wounds may find themselves more capable of forming connections with others. This can manifest as improved communication skills, increased trust in others, and a reduced tendency to isolate oneself. A healed individual is often more open to intimacy and can set healthy boundaries.

Empowerment and Agency – Healing allows individuals to regain a sense of control over their lives. They may begin to feel empowered to make choices that align with their values and desires, rather than reacting to past trauma. This sense of agency is often accompanied by setting and achieving personal goals, a renewed motivation for life, and a clearer understanding of their identity.

Coping Mechanisms and Resilience – Another sign of healing is the development of effective coping strategies. Individuals may notice that they are more resilient in the face of stress. They can manage challenges without reverting to old, unhealthy coping mechanisms like substance abuse or self-harm. Instead, they engage in healthier activities such as exercise, mindfulness, or creative expression.

Increased Self-Compassion – A crucial aspect of healing is the ability to practice self-compassion. As individuals heal, they often become less critical of themselves and more understanding of their experiences. They recognize that healing takes time and that setbacks are a natural part of the process. This shift in mindset fosters a more positive self-image and the ability to forgive oneself for past mistakes.

Reflection and Insight – Healing can lead to deeper self-reflection and insight into one's experiences. Individuals may understand the impact of their trauma on their lives and develop a new perspective that allows them to find meaning in their experiences. This ability to reflect often results in a transformative narrative that emphasizes growth rather than victimization.

Interest in New Experiences – Finally, those who have healed from past traumas often find themselves more open to new experiences. They may feel a desire to explore new relationships, hobbies, or objectives that they previously shied away from due to fear or anxiety. This openness signifies a restored sense of curiosity and engagement with life.

Recognizing that you have healed from past hurts and trauma is ultimately about self-awareness and the ability to perceive changes in your thoughts, emotions, and behaviors. While the healing journey can be tumultuous, the signs mentioned above can serve as markers of progress. It's important to remember that healing is not about forgetting the past but rather about learning to integrate those experiences in a way that fosters well-being and resilience. Each person's journey is unique and embracing it with patience and compassion is key to lasting healing.

Session 6 Questions

Please use extra paper if needed.

Signs of Healing:
1. What are some indicators or signs in your life that make you feel you have healed from a past hurt?

Emotional Shifts:
2. How have your emotions changed regarding a particular hurtful experience?
3. Are there moments when you feel at peace about it?

Triggers:
4. Have you noticed any changes in how you respond to triggers related to your past experiences?
5. How do you handle those triggers now?

Perspective Change:
6. In what ways has your perspective on the hurtful experience evolved over time?
7. What do you now understand that you didn't before?

Relationships:
8. How has your healing impacted your relationships with others?
9. Do you feel different in how you connect or communicate

with friends and loved ones?

Self-Compassion:

10. How do you practice self-compassion now compared to before your healing journey?
11. What does it look like for you?

Reflective Practices:

12. Have you engaged in any reflective practices (like journaling or meditation) to assess your healing?
13. What insights have you gained from them?

Future Concerns:

14. How do you feel about facing similar situations or feelings in the future? Do you feel more equipped to handle them?

Gratitude:

15. In what ways do you express gratitude for your healing journey?
16. How has gratitude played a role in your process?

Supportive Environment:

17. How has being part of a supportive community influenced your healing process?
18. How can we continue to support each other in recognizing our healing?

Use the following pages for your answers:

Session

7

Avoid Being a Dumping Ground During your Healing Process

Session 7

In our interconnected world, it is common for individuals to seek support from friends, family, and colleagues when facing challenges. situations can arise where one person becomes overwhelmed by the constant stream of other's troubles often referred to as being a dumping ground for their issues.

To maintain healthy relationships and emotional wellbeing, it is essential to establish boundaries and cultivate strategies that enable individuals to support others without becoming emotionally depleted.

Understanding the Dynamics of Emotional Dumping

Emotional dumping occurs when a person unloads their problems onto someone else, often without consideration for that person's emotional state or capacity to help. This can manifest as a one-sided conversation where the listener feels pressured to absorb and validate the speaker's issues, leading to a feeling of stress, frustration, or helplessness.

Understanding this dynamic pave the way for recognizing when it occurs and how to address it constructively.

Establishing Healthy Boundaries

One of the most effective ways to avoid being a dumping ground is to establish clear boundaries. This involves communicating to others how much emotional labor you are willing to engage in and recognizing your own limits. Setting boundaries can include:

- **Defining Time Limits** – Allocating specific times for conversations about personal issues can help manage expectations and limit unexpected emotional heavy-lifting.
- **Encouraging Self-Sufficiency** – Instead of providing solutions, encourage others to think critically about their problems and explore potential solutions themselves. This fosters independence and reduces reliance on you as a continuous source of support.
- **Being Honest About Your Emotions** – If you feel overwhelmed, it's important to communicate this to others. Let them know you need time to process your own feelings before you can effectively support anyone else.

Employing Active Listening Techniques

While it is important to protect one's emotional wellbeing, employing active listening strategies can allow for supportive interactions without becoming overwhelmed. Active listening involves being fully present in conversations and showing empathy without absorbing the emotional burden. Techniques include:

- **Reflective Feedback** – Paraphrase what the speaker is saying to show understanding without taking on their emotions.
- **Asking Open Ended Questions** – Prompt them to explore their feelings and thoughts independently.
- **Validating Feelings** – Acknowledge their emotions to make them feel heard without diving deep into the emotional aspect yourself.

Navigating relationships where emotional dumping occurs does not have to be detrimental to one's mental health. By establishing boundaries, employing active listening techniques, encouraging professional help, and practicing self-care, individuals can create a balance that fosters supportive relationships without becoming overwhelmed. In this way, we not only help those around us but also ensure that we do not lose sight of our own emotional needs. Remember you are going through a healing process yourself. On another note, you can just simply refer them to this book and share your experiences you had thus far.

Session 7 Questions

Please use extra paper if needed.

1. What does it mean for you to create a safe and supportive environment without feeling overwhelmed?
2. How can we prioritize our own healing while being supportive to others?
3. What strategies can we implement to maintain healthy boundaries within our group?
4. How can we encourage members to express their feelings without turning the discussions into solely venting sessions?
5. What are some signs that a conversation is becoming a dumping ground and how can we address it?
6. How can we balance sharing experiences and providing solutions in our discussions?
7. In what ways can we structure our meetings to promote positive dialogue and mutual support?
8. How do you feel after a group discussion, and what could we do to ensure everyone leaves feeling uplifted?

9. What role does active listening play in our conversations, and how can we practice it while ensuring we don't absorb negativity?
10. Can you identify practices or rituals to help transition into a more positive mindset before our discussions begin.

Use the following pages for your answers:

Session

8

Support Systems

Session 8

The Importance of Community and Support Systems

Support systems are crucial for emotional and psychological well-being. They consist of people, groups, or resources that provide assistance, encouragement, and understanding during difficult times. Here are various types of support systems and ideas for building and maintaining them.

Types of Support Systems

- ▸ *Family and Friends* – Close relationships with family members or friends who can offer emotional support, practical help, and companionship.

- ▸ *Professional Support* – Mental Health professionals (therapists, counselors) who provide guidance and coping strategies for emotional challenges.

- ▸ *Support Groups* – Groups where individuals with similar experiences (e.g, grief, illness, addiction) gather to share and support each other, fostering a sense of community.

- ▸ *Community Resources* – Local organizations, non-profits, or religious groups that offer support services, workshops, and social activities.

- ▸ *Online Communities* – Virtual forums or social media groups where people share, seek advice, and provide support. Examples include Reddit, Facebook groups, or specialized forums.

- ***Workplace Support*** – Employee assistance programs (EAPs), mentoring, or supportive colleagues can be essential for managing stress related to career challenges.

Building a Support System – Building and maintaining strong community support networks can lead to improved social cohesion and overall quality of life. Individuals are encouraged to seek out and engage with their communities to foster these supportive relationships.

Embracing the Journey from Hurt to Healing

As we come to the end of this journey together, it's important to recognize that healing is not a destination but a continuous process, one filled with triumphs, setbacks, and profound growth. Each chapter of our lives tells a story, and while the scars of hurt may always remain, they can become symbols of resilience and strength. Remember, the courage to confront your pain is the first step towards reclaiming your life. You have embarked on a journey of self-discovery, weaving through the shadows of your past and emerging with a newfound sense of self-awareness and empowerment.

As you take your next steps, hold tight to the lessons learned and the relationships nurtured along the way. Healing is personal; honor your timeline and give yourself grace. Surround yourself with supportive communities, continue to cultivate self-love, and be open to the beauty that lies ahead.

May you always find the light within, even on the darkest days. Trust that every step forward, no matter how small, brings you closer to your true self. Here's to the ongoing chapters of your life, may they be filled with hope, healing, and endless possibilities.

Thank you for allowing me to be part of your journey. You are not alone, and your story is far from over. Embrace your healing, and let it guide you toward a future filled with joy and fulfillment.

A Personal Prayer For You

Dear God,

In times of hurt and pain, we turn to You as our source of comfort and strength. We acknowledge our struggles, the wounds that weigh heavy on our hearts, and the scars that remind us of difficult times.

We ask for Your healing touch to mend our brokenness, to soothe our spirits, and to restore us to wholeness. Help us to release our burdens and to find peace in the midst of turmoil. Surround us with Your loving presence, and grant us the courage to face our challenges with faith.

As we journey toward healing, may we also extend grace and forgiveness to ourselves and others, freeing our hearts from the chains of resentment and despair.

Guide us towards a path of restoration, where we can reclaim joy, hope, and purpose in our lives. Thank You for Your unconditional love and for the promise of renewal. May we emerge stronger and more resilient, ready to embrace the future with open hearts.

In Jesus Name Amen.

Prophet Gail Hurt is a loving mother who entered her God-ordained calling as a Prophetic Intercessor in 2012. Her mission is to pursue and walk in God's purpose, leaving no man behind through teaching, coaching, engaging, and encouraging others to believe in the possibilities. She focuses on women of all ages who have lost their way, resuscitating, rejuvenating, and restoring them to life with a foundation rooted and grounded in Christ Jesus.

Omaha, Nebraska

Testimonials

Being apart of Hurt to Healing Transformation Center has truly changed my life. It is run by a beautiful woman named Gail and she is anointed and carries the holy spirit with her wherever she goes. I know if I need guidance she's there and if she doesn't have the answer, she will do what she can to find it. There are few people like her in the world and her ministry has truly changed my life. I always look forward to our weekly meetings because I always learn something new. Gail nature is loving and kind she's very encouraging and patient, it's truly a blessing to have encountered such a beautiful woman of God, to know her is to love her.

Trina Jenkins

Gail is generous in reminding me of who I am (a child of God). She inspires me to live life and find my purpose, she has encouraged me to fulfill hidden talents and strengths and weaknesses in my life through the Hurt to Healing Transformation Center. Her love and care is what she has given me, to think with a positive mindset and the tools to better strive in life. Thank you, Gail, for being my coach!

Sherene Carter

www.ingramcontent.com/pod-product-compliance
Lightning Source LLC
Chambersburg PA
CBHW071227160426
43196CB00012B/2444